To Grief with Love
A lyrical and pictorial voyage through loss

ZOE STRICKLAND

'Zoe shares her journey with loss and grief with such openness, honesty and compassion. Her drawings speak volumes where words can so often fail; her words have an utterly relatable truth and wisdom in them; both come together like a supportive hand offered in a dark and painful time. 'To Grief with Love' is a beautiful gift of healing and comfort; a valuable companion on a difficult path we will all ultimately share.'
– Philip Carr-Gomm, Author of 'The Gift of the Night: A Six Step Program for Better Sleep' –

"Nourishment for the soul."
– Jo O'Callaghan, Transpersonal psychotherapist –

"Beautiful words. Zoe's book holds such compassion and wisdom. I love her writings."
– Debbie Savage, Natural therapies practitioner –

"This book will provide comfort to those who experience loss in a multitude of ways, and will allow a glimpse into this world for those who need to provide support to others."
– Amanda Roberts – General Practitioner –

"This beautiful book will be valued not just by those experiencing grief, but also therapists working with grief. It really is an extraordinary expression of feeling and experience."
– Sophie Fletcher - Clinical Hypnotherapist, author and trainer –

"This book has helped me today. Sudden and totally unexpected bereavement yesterday of my very close childhood friend. In Sydney. Same gang. Many memories."
– Gill McNeil –

"This is absolutely beautiful and wise."
– Dagmar Hirsch, Yoga teacher –

"A sensitive narrative of grief. Thanks for sharing."
– Catherine McInerny Pregnancy Massage Australia –

"I love Zoe's visual – simple but powerful and true."
– Sue Koelle –

"So beautifully articulated."
– Emma Dare –

"Zoe, your son has opened for you an amazing journey through which you are touching many other hearts."
– Jana Silk –

"Such beautiful reflections."
– Student Grief Network –

"Wonderful and precious insights and gifts to share with others."
– Sue Wilson –

"Zoe's work inspires me, leaves me in awe of what humans can cope with."
– Kym Fullerton –

"Well I just read it in one sitting. It is extremely moving, extremely honest and extremely uplifting – I had tears running down my face – but I was not overwhelmed, nor did I sob. The thing I love most is the magic that is present! I recognized much and much resonated. How amazing Zoe has created this."
– Sarah Barker Brown, Artist –

"Zoe's writing is so beautiful, gentle and painful, yet never overly self-indulgent - the doodles are so breathtakingly expressive they are brilliant."
– Nick Leslau –

"Thank you, thank you. The most powerful thing is the honesty and integrity with which you share yourself. There is not a single hint of self pity, so its immediately universal."
– Diane Finlay, Author –

To Grief with Love
© Zoe Strickland 2024

All rights reserved. No part of this publication may be reproduced, stored in a retrieval system, or transmitted in any form or by any means, electronic, mechanical, photocopying, recording or otherwise, without the prior written permission of the author.

ISBN: 978-1-7638300-0-4 (hardcover) 97978-1-7638300-1-1 (paperback)

 A catalogue record for this book is available from the National Library of Australia

Lead editor: Kym Fullerton
Copy editor: Marisa Parker
Printed in Australia
Published by Zoe Strickland Publishing
www.zoestricklandpublishing.com

I wrote this for me

I share it for us

us who mourn our loved ones

us who are learning to carry our grief

as well as living our best lives.

I share to give grief a voice

a grief odyssey

an ode to grief

an ode to love.

In memory of our beloved Elliot,

And dedicated to my anchors in LOVE,

David, Jacob, and Freddy.

Prelude

Dear Reader,

If you are holding this book in your hands, it is likely you are mourning the loss of a person you love, and I connect my heart up to yours in compassion. Grief hurts so much, it's hard to carry, and can be such a lonely business.

I am sorry for your loss.

The day my own universe tilted was an ordinary Friday. Everything seemed well, and then it wasn't. Because that night, our beautiful eldest son, twenty-five years young, unimaginably, unbelievably, and unpredictably, took his life.

Five years on, it's still hard to say that. And as I sit, pen in hand, deciding what to write by way of an introduction, Elliot's lovely face appears in my mind's eye, there is a familiar lump in my throat, a familiar tightening around my heart, and a squeeze on my soul. I expect you know just what I mean.

On that tragic day, June 23rd 2018, I felt a biological rupture. A splitting into two—into myself, and my grief self. I started a diary. I journaled fervently. It was an outlet for the darkness, to let my pen scream, to hurl poetry at the universe. Those secret pages were also keepers of comforting wisdoms, texts, words, quotes or podcasts that found me.

I kept two diaries, one for me and another to write to Elliot. I still do. I wanted to keep the dark stuff out of his. It's a meeting place where I chat to him, tell him I love him, ask for guidance, give him family news, record felt synchronicities, symbolisms, musings, dreams. Anything I fancy, really.

And *Doodle Lady* was born.

She wasn't a conscious birthing. She was an arising from the depths. She who could depict my innards when words were too wordy. She who could express my grief self, so I could carry on being me. Grief was my mess. It also became my message as I started to share Doodle Lady posts. I have such admiration for the millions who quietly go about their grief … when I have felt the need to shout about mine.

I could readily have titled this work, *Dear Grief What the F**k!* such is the awful pain, chaos, despair … and a million other adjectives that accompany the anguish of early traumatic grief. Yet, somewhere deep inside my core, I made a pact with myself, that though my life was damaged, and would never be the same, I was going to survive, for me, for Elliot, for my family, for others. Because we must, and we can.

The more fiercely we love, the more fiercely we grieve, and though my fighting spirit set intention, my biggest grief-learning has been that She asks for a gentle suturing of the heart, the soul, and the psyche. A letting go of why? Why? Why? Some things just can't be fixed in the head, and so the title, more intuitively, became *To Grief with Love*.

It was never my intention to write a book. This work is a collection of diary entries, lyrical and pictorial expressions of my thoughts and feelings in the undertow. I wrote this for myself, and Doodle Lady speaks for me, yet I think she speaks for us all too. We trek such similar paths in all our humanness.

There is darkness in these pages. I include not to vent or to shock, but to be truthful. I'm sure you will relate. There is also a sweeter song, because the light and the dark sit together. Unexpected treasure was found as Doodle Lady journeyed in. Grief learnings, life learnings, death learnings. She found a portal to hope, possibility, and wonder. She found solace in divinity, as an experience, not as a handing over. And all of this in no particular order. The road to healing is never linear.

The day of our loss seems forever ago, and yet just a blink in time. Living with hard grief is like having a dual life. The one I thought I knew, and the one I have been learning to live now. It's not easy, but I have arrived at a place where there is more equilibrium, and where there are fewer snakes and ladders. We've been learning to live together—Doodle Lady and I. Now we can pull up a chair next to each other at the table, and in doing so, we come together in the sharing of this diary.

Our experiences of grief are as individual as we are. I share my diaries not as a self-help or how-to-do-grief guide. I share my soul words in the spirit of giving grief a voice, and to connect in compassion with others who may be suffering too, so they don't feel alone. And perhaps through the grace of the divine smithy, I have been able to forge my grief from molten sorrow into something useful.

I offer *To Grief with Love*, as a tending and befriending of grief, a partnering, a wafting of the flickering embers that sustain our inner pilot light, so we may carry on a life rich in meaning and purpose.

A sojourn in grief.

An eternity in love.

Contents

The doodles throughout this book, tell of my grief from my journals, as it unfolded. In bringing this work together, I added accompanying narrative, to expand a little, to proffer things that helped, and to share quotations I liked from other authors.

You might wander these pages in sequence, or dip in and out. I have indexed the doodles with page numbers to make it easier to re-visit a page, share it, or perhaps doodle your own thoughts.

But there is no *progression*. There is just the swash and the backwash, the rough and the smooth, the sadness and periods of steady in between. Because it's like that, grief, isn't it? And though there is no conclusion, because the apprenticeship continues, I notice in myself a softening at the end of this round of journaling, mirroring my state of being.

 I sincerely wish this for you too.

In the resources section, I reference books, meditations, and courses that inspired and comforted. Some found me, and some were shared with me. I pass on these wisdoms; I pass on the torch, so that we all might pass them on, and shine a little brighter on our darker days.

Doodles in Sequence

HANGING ON	14
TRAPPED	16
STANDING IN THE RAIN	18
HOPE	20
GRIEF SHOCK	22
I CALL YOUR NAME	26

THE GRIEF ROOM DOOR	28
COMPASSION	30
TIGHTROPE	32
GUILT	34
BOTTOMLESS	36
AN ANGEL WITH THEIR NAME	38
WALKING TOGETHER	40
SLOW LANE	42
STUCK	44
BIRD SONGS	46
PEN FRIENDS	48
ON YOUR BIRTHDAY	49
MARY POPPINS	50
MAD DANCING	52
MASCARA	54
BEWARE THE DROP OFF	56
ALCOHOL	58
FFS	59
GRIEF FURROWS	60
BLACK DOG	62
WHERE ARE YOU?	64
LITTLE THINGS THAT LIFT	66

HELLO GRIEF WHAT DO YOU NEED TODAY	68
DO MORE LITTLE THINGS THAT LIFT	69
STAGES OF GRIEF	71
FAITH	72
BRACE BRACE	74
QUICKSAND	76
MAKING TEA	78
TREADING ON EGGSHELLS	80
STAR GAZING	81
IS THIS BARGAINING?	82
JOY ENVY	84
'I VANT TO BE ALONE'	87
BOXING GLOVES	88
HOLLOW	90
TO BE OR NOT TO BE	92
NIGHT VISION	94
HUNTER MOON	96
MAY, PLEASE STAY	98
ON LONGING	101
EAGLE POEMS	103
YOUR ANNIVERSARY	104
ON TALKING TO EAGLES	106

AND SOMETIMES	108
SECRET WORLD	110
SPLIFEROONY	112
FOG CLEARING	114
PADDED QUILT SKIES	116
GRIEF / LOVE	117
I PRAY	118
CORONER'S LETTER	119
DIVING BACK INTO THERAPY	122
HELPFUL/ UNHELPFUL	124
ON NATURE	126
LIGHTNESS OF BEING	128
UPSIDE DOWN	130
IMAGINARY WINGS	132
MAGIC HAPPENS	134
UNDER BELLY	136
I ACKNOWLEDGE	137
WORK, WORK, WORK	138
HUMPTY	140
PARACELSUS	142
KINTSUGI	144
MAKING FRIENDS WITH THE MOON	146

START WHERE YOU ARE	148
A LETTER TO SUFFERING	150
LAUNDRY	152
POSTLUDE	154
RESOURCES	156
ACKNOWLEDGMENTS	158

My first doodle. The first wake up. Oh God!

The realisation that grips your chest, thumps you in the throat. You feel nauseous, spacey, unreal, but reality lurks right alongside.

Hang on to anything you can and just keep hanging on.

I get up, move body, have a shower, eat if I don't feel too sick, arrange flowers, sleep, light candles, arrange more flowers … on repeat. Something in the caring intention, the routine/ritual of sorts, the smell of the wax, the colours of the flowers, brought me comfort. We snuggled with the dog. My husband found distraction in grocery shopping.

I'm forever grateful for the food that he had the care, love, and presence to make us in amongst his own darkest hours.

Our boys slept, watched telly, cuddled with their girlfriends, made pumpkin soup, cut the grass, cuddled their girlfriends some more. We moved around the house like bewildered zombies. The dog was sad. The silence only punctuated with hugs. Words not necessary now.

Hang on to anything you can. Please trust it softens.

Trapped in a frustration that can't be righted.

A flame of grief you ignited.

I could have helped.

This didn't have to be …

I am bereft.

Poor me.

Standing in the rain

I am blessed to have people that will stand in the rain with me and are prepared to get wet.

On a difficult day, these words came right back at me, in a text. My friend's steady shoulders and warm heart, available to me at any time. Find this person, or these people. Stay close to them.

People surprised me. Some I thought could be there for me in the way I needed, but just weren't. No judgement … it's just how it is.

Others enter your world serendipitously.

Grief, it's a fickle business.

Standing with someone in the rain requires empathy and long-term consistency. Umbrella to hand.

Dear Reader, I hope you sense me, here, standing in the rain with you.

Hope
Offers
Possibilities
Everyday

Hope

I find unsolicited positivity such a betrayal of grief. Such an insult. But through some divine act of mercy, I do feel hope. Hope as an intention and as a state of the heart. The flickering pilot light that sustains me from deep inside. I sincerely wish everyone much hope.

> *Hope is the ingredient that supplies the motivation to get us up in the morning and look forward to the possibilities of a new day. I think of hope as an active, open trust in life that refuses to quit. Hope takes us beyond rational. It is an abiding state of being, a hidden wellspring within us. We can sense the lightness and buoyancy with this kind of hope. It energizes us to engage in activities that we imagine will enrich our future. This version of hope is a basic human need.*
>
> —Frank Ostaseski, *The Five Invitations.*
> *(Discovering what dying can teach us about living fully in the present).*

Grief shock

My brain doesn't have any frame of reference for this. There is bewilderment—also a weird endorphin response which feels dreamy, almost euphoric—but a simultaneous unfathomable terribleness somewhere, just out there. I'm on autopilot … an ability to be quite functional in discussing "it", almost with detachment, yet totally dysfunctional in most other practical ways.

Physically—muscle aches, fatigue, brain fog, constant nausea, headache, tight heart, I'm talking fast, rapid heart rate, then so slow. Am I dead?

I'm walking between two worlds—mine and Elliot's—a liminal space somewhere between dreaming and waking. Still connected, the cord not yet cut. Perhaps they stay really close right now, partnering us, sending coping tactics for our soul?

I felt so intuitive in early loss. Especially around what felt right for his funeral, and what didn't. Like when you have a newborn. You know what you want. Who you want around you. Who can handle your child, or your loved person.

Don't entertain niceties or do anything you don't want to. Listen to advice but allow your instincts to be your guide.

Allow a village to gather around you.

It is likely to be a different village than the one you're used to.

I call your name.

My voice

a primal scream

cracks open the brittle shell of my outer being

and my sorrow, my insides

seep out

till I'm drained flat.

I call your name.

Frustration …

a force so intense it could split the atom

or grip the universe like a mighty god

and hurl it in into

rewind rewind rewind.

"Where are you?"

I shout your name out loud
It's shocking but feels good to hear
to get it out.

I call your name

I grasp the air, hug the space—can you hear me? Are you listening? I miss saying your name. I miss hearing your name. So, I scream it out: "ELLIOT!" This makes me cry. And then …

Yes! I know you can hear me; I know you are listening.
I smile, because now I feel you say, "Mum, there's no need to shout!"

Later that day, I opened a book, and just the right words found me …

> *Right now, I am not these eyes, I am loving awareness.*
>
> *Right now, I am not these ears and these sounds, I am loving awareness.*
>
> *I am not this mouth, this talking, this tasting, I am loving awareness.*
>
> *I am not this body, these sensations, this touch, I am loving awareness.*
>
> *I rest from inside out in loving awareness.*
>
> *My soul continues forever in loving awareness.*
>
> —Ram Dass.

The Grief Room door

After two weeks, I started my first psychotherapy sessions with Jo. She was also our celebrant. There was a feeling of familiarity as she walked through our garden gate, and we knew instantly that something special had brought her into our lives.

Early grief was terrifying. I called it my Grief Room. I daren't go in. I saw a bottomless hollow place behind the door, beyond words, beyond tears, beyond possible.

Jo encouraged me to open the door. "Just a little. Get a bit of light in there, a bit of fresh air. There you go … pouf, pouf." She blew gently and wafted the air around in a kind way. "Do you want to take a wise being in with you?" she asked. "For protection?" And he arrived in my mind, by my side, at the door. It was Gandalf the Grey—powerful, supportive, and magical.

Psyche means soul or consciousness. The in-dweller or animating principal that houses the physical body and directs us. The word is also derived from the Greek word for breath, *pneuma,* and the Sanskrit word, *prana.* In Greek mythology, Psyche (Psykhe) was the goddess of the soul. She was born mortal, with magical powers of flight, immortality, and unrivalled beauty. Despite all this, she was sad, because she was unloved. Her story is about the soul redeeming itself through love.

I love this story. And with help, I learned to breathe love into my psyche, into my soul, and into grief. And although I found myself in the darkest of times, the Grief Room became a portal; a door to another universe. One of metaphor, symbolism, and experiences of divine partnering. A place where I learned more about life, love, and death than the fifty-seven years that preceded. Where I learned to get out of the way of my mind and attend to the gentle caring of my heart.

> *Open the door and step out. The path will become visible. On the way you will meet other wayfarers who will advise and guide you. Your job is to muster whatever strength you have to get underway. Thereafter help is assured.*
>
> —Sri Anandamayi Ma.

I take a deep bow to the measure of my suffering and that of others ..... compassion

Compassion

Week Two

How the hell does the world function with all these people simultaneously carrying so much grief? How do people show up to work and carry on their day? Get the groceries? Care for their others? Care for themselves? How does the world keep spinning?

I find little things so irritating, big things so draining. I just want to sleep. And how dare they push in front of me in the supermarket queue … don't they know? Maybe there should be some internationally recognised armband we wear that says, "I'm grieving, be kind."

And I felt compassion like I had never felt before. Deep respect, deep empathy. The normalcy of death, it washes over, until it doesn't.

"I'm so very sorry for your loss."

I enrolled straight away into an exquisitely comforting heart-based mindfulness course with Jack Kornfield. A weekly beacon in the dark. Like taking a warm shower in human kindness.

I gradually came to understand that when my mind screams over and over, "How can I bear this?"

My heart replies, "Just listen to me dear." x

I inch along the tightrope. The bottom is a long way down, I don't know where it stops, but I trust angel wings will lift me when I lose concentration and wobble.

Tightrope

I wondered …

How far am I going to fall?

How deep the abyss?

But something happened early on—it wasn't cerebral, it just happened. It was a 'felt' sense. A trust that I could bear it. That I was being carried by something bigger. A kind and benevolent power. Perhaps, in the early fog of grief, somewhere softly embedded in our DNA, spiralled in our encoded wisdom, we *do* understand. A soul remembering? So, I inch slowly along.

Please trust you can carry this, and you will be carried.

Guilt

If only I had known … I would have tucked you up in bed for three weeks, made you chicken soup. If only I had known.

So many what ifs, regrets, moments I wish I'd been more present, soaked up more of our time together, deeper listening, made that trip we were planning, told you not to worry about anything.

I learned there is pain in grief, and there is suffering. Guilt is suffering.

You have to work very hard not to go down that rabbit hole because it lures you in, swallows you up. Be vigilant. Back up when guilt beckons. Get someone else to remind you, often.

I learned a mantra for guilty thoughts and self-talk.

"Is this true? Is this helpful? Is this kind?"

Bottomless

Week Four

I'm so cold. I feel sick. I have hiccups. It's not getting better. Grief's getting worse, darker, sadder, hopeless … a bottomless well.

I'm encouraged to circle gently around the edge, take little peeks. I don't have to look in right now. When I'm ready, I take a torch. And as my eyes adjust to the dark, I see little ledges along the walls where I can sit and rest. I see it's not bottomless, there's no hard landing. It opens up into spaciousness … and you are with me in the spaciousness.

When the clouds of grief part
those we love but physically lost
to us, come to us as angels –
directing us in love and compassion
to tune in to our higher selves
our own personal angel
with their name
This I know

An angel with their name

Dear Elliot, do you remember the lovely Indian lady and her husband that live over the road? I don't know her very well … other than to wave over the fence when we take Chubbs for a walk. I met her in the park. She came over, gave me a most deep hug. She patted my tight heart, smiled, and said with the kindest brown eyes, and in such a matter-of-fact way …

"Try to relax, daaarling … you'll make it easier for him, you'll see, it's going to be okay."

Gear change! Easier for *him* to continue on his healing journey? Easier for *him* to come through? And it was so. When my energy is less dense, and grief softer, I feel him; I feel him closer, relaxing and healing. And we became open to incredulous synchronicity, which I continue to journal. A diary entry from a couple of weeks in: *Elliot, I'm going to have to get a bloody secretary the messages are coming so thick and fast! Thank you. Love you x.*

The connection with spirit … it became a 'knowing' above wishful thinking. A knowing above wondering. A knowing above belief … that we are always connected in Oneness. I feel him as my guide, like a rudder. I ask, and feel answers … in dreams, on walks, in nature's messages, in feathers, in eagles, in tree frogs sitting on my husband's brew spoon, in songs, in car regos, in table numbers. When I stay in the love lane.

> *It is only with the heart that we can rightly see.*
>
> *What is essential, is invisible to the eye.*
>
> —Antoine de Saint-Exupéry, *The Little Prince.*

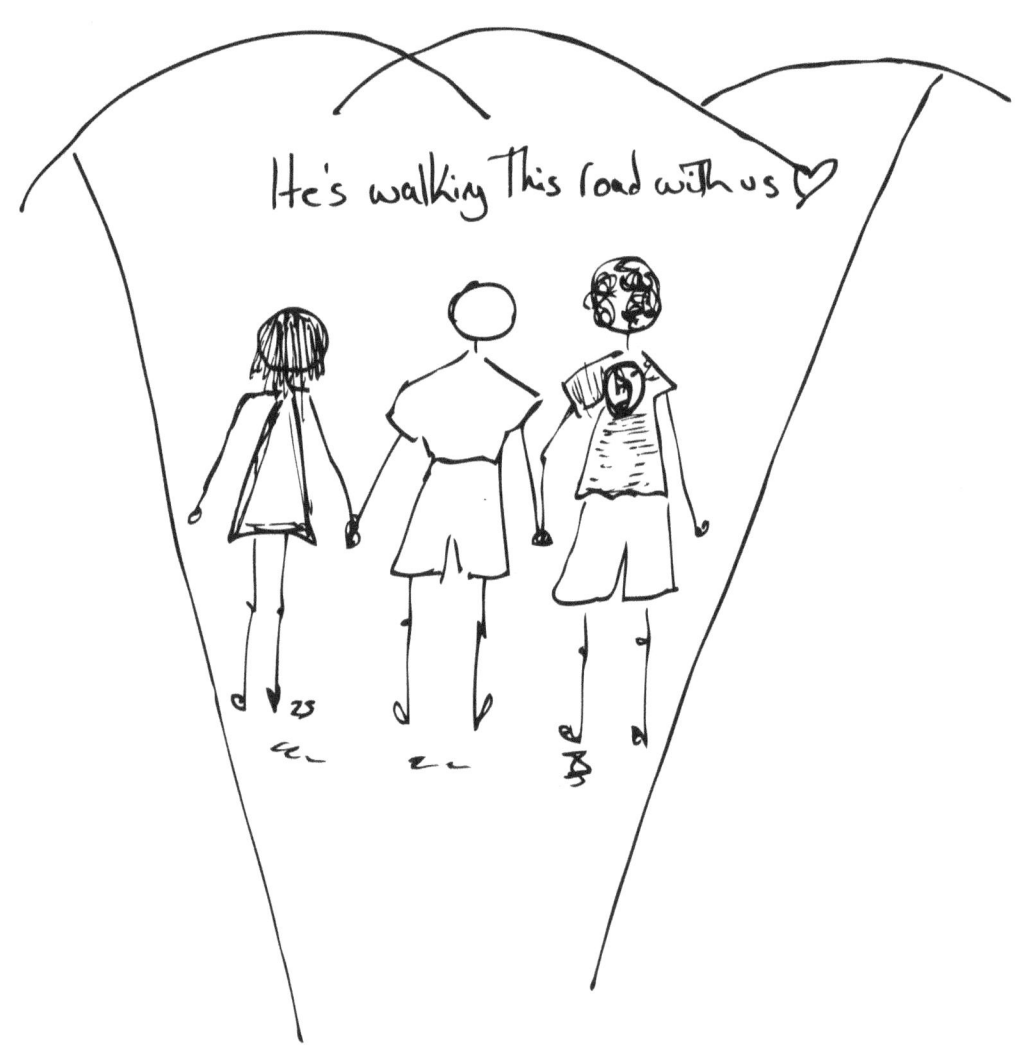

Walking together

Week Five

Dear Debi,

David and I feel such a strong sense that we are walking this together.

> *When we are open to it, love is everywhere, and those who we love who are no longer physically with us – are always available to us, especially when we use our love for them as compassion, and let it flow and return to us as self-compassion. What would they do? What would they want for us in this moment? His love and guidance is always there when we are present, we just have to access it in a new way.*
>
> —Debi x
> (Debi Roberts, dear family friend and CEO of The OLLIE Foundation.
> One Life Lost Is Enough).

I notice when I'm being too
busy, going too fast,
and get back in the slow lane.
The slow lane always best
in unknown terrain.

Slow lane

"We go slow on a bumpy road, don't we?" counselled my therapist.

She said move slowly, take baths, wear loose clothes, pad gently in sheepskin slippers, sleep in soft sheets, accept help. For we trip up if we go too fast … too quickly or hurl ourselves into distraction.

It is so true. First aid for the soul is best administered in the slow lane.

What does my slow lane look like?

Rituals slow me down. They are a bridge to peace. Family-favourite meals at home, walks in the park with our beloved Chubbs (our dog), walks along the beach, gentle exercise, less talking, more being. Meditating, listening to mantras, being quiet, pottering around, making wands and smudge bundles, tending the garden, reading, doodling, doing things that help me feel peaceful.

I'm happiest when I'm being a snail.

Stuck

Today, I'm stuck.

"It's OKAY not to be OKAY," is *not* helping.

body so heavy

head foggy

mood flat

can't lift

so …

tired.

Find someone to talk to, to walk with.

Sometimes the simplest thing is the hand that pulls you out. A hand that pulls you out without any accompanying fuss or drama. A helpful reframe, a visualisation, an inspiring book. A hand attached to a person with deep listening. A person who has been in a dark place themselves … a person who knows.

As time goes on, it's harder to ask. But keep asking.

> *A problem aired is a problem shared, dear.*
> —Nana, Muriel.

I went to sleep to the curlews' call

the spirit of souls wanting to be reborn

the sound of the dead returning to the dreaming

and the cries of mothers who have lost their children …

they forever mourn.

I woke

to the song of the "chung chung" bird

their call and response

a prayer

aerial communication

a reminder there is a language other than the one we know.

Pen friends

Messaging is sometimes easier than speaking.

I'm so grateful for my pen friends. Some live near, some far away, and some further still, overseas. The time difference between hemispheres was helpful for once, providing a lifeline deep into the night. Some were from lived-experience groups, grief chatrooms, or suicide bereavement support groups.

In those early days, the little backwards and forwards exchanges, when I simply could not sleep, were a lifeline.

Messaging allows you to dip in and out. Gives you more control. Longer pauses. Often you don't want the commitment of a face-to-face conversation. No eye contact … what a blessed relief.

It's not shallow to want this.

On your birthday

July 23rd 2018

It's your birthday. Your first in heaven.

Debbie bought us a crystal singing bowl. It sits on your table, and we ding it as we walk past. It seems Love has a sound! The miracle note. 528Hz. The note of F. I googled … you'll love this!

The ancient yogis knew that the F note resonates at the heart of all people and the frequency of 528Hz was used by ancient healers and priests in the civilisations of Mesoamerica, Europe, and Australia.

Scientist Victor Showell describes the frequency of 528Hz as being fundamental to Pi and the Golden Mean, evident throughout natural design, and essential to the sacred geometry of circles and spirals. The vibrations of F during sound healing bring peace and harmony, restoring equilibrium to everyone and everything around it.

I feel you most when I tune in to the vibration of LOVE—528Hz X

Everything is possible, even the impossible.

—Mary Poppins.
(Character of book by the same name, Australian-British writer, P L Travers).

Mary Poppins

My sister came over from the UK, three months after your passing. She breezed in on a North wind. Got in our lane with us. Kept us steady. Made us profiteroles. She's my Mary Poppins. It's a long way to Cairns from the UK, a long trip for a week, though we shared much presence, much quality time. The mad dancing was a highlight! Yes, there was much merriment, even amongst it all. Miss you Mary Poppins. See you soon. x

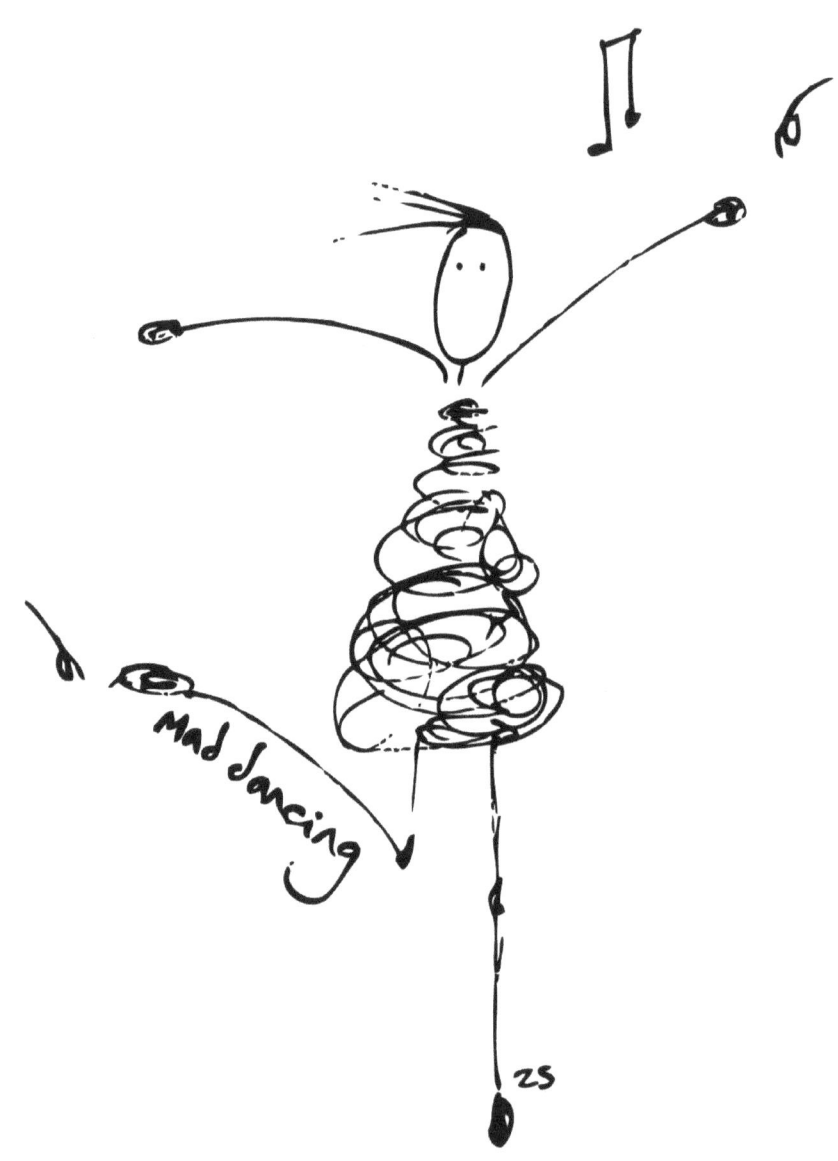

Mad dancing

... two whirling dervishes out the back, a bottle of red, David as DJ, taking us through the 70s, 80s ... I kind of remember getting to the 90s (?), and all the while, your joyful photo, 'double-parked in Bali' ... your full body smile was watching us, joining us. Enjoying our crazy!

Mascara

One morning, about six months in, I woke up actually feeling good for a change. So, I told myself, "Zoe, get some nice clothes on … accessorise… put makeup on … call a friend … meet for coffee … and talk about something else!"

I cried over coffee and went to buy waterproof mascara!

bobbing around in the gentle swash and backwash is better. Like a cork dip lightly and pop back to the surface

Beware the drop off

I notice I function better in quietude, in a calm natural environment, one with few people in it. Gentle social activities that involve *doing*. A shoulder-to-shoulder walk, playing scrabble, watching a band, crafting. The lows seem to be lower after the highs ... steady feels better.

Beware the drop off.

There's a long way to fall after the high waves. I beware the drop off

Alcohol is not helpful to grief. There is always a spike in my sad-o-meter after drinking alcohol. Just a glass of wine, or two or three … a brief lift, up the windward slope … then a slide down the leeward.

Note to self. Alcohol is not helpful when you are sad. It's a depressant.

F word F word F word F word F word F word F word F word F word F word F word F word
F word F word F word F word F word F word F word F word F word F word F word F word
F word F word F word F word F word F word F word F word F word F word F word F word
F word F word F w   vord F word F word
F word F word F w   vord F word F word
F word F word F w   word F word F word
F word F word F w   word F word F word
F word F word F w   word F word F word
F word F word F w   word F word F word
F word F word F w   word F word F word
F word F word F w   word F word F word
F word F word F w   word F word F word
F word F word F w   word F word F word
F word F word F w   word F word F word
F word F word F w   word F word F word
F word F word F w   word F word F word
F word F word F w   word F word F word
F word F word F w   word F word F word
F word F word F v   word F word F word
F word F word F word F word F word F word F word F word F word F word F word F word

f.f.s.

Sometimes there's only one word for it

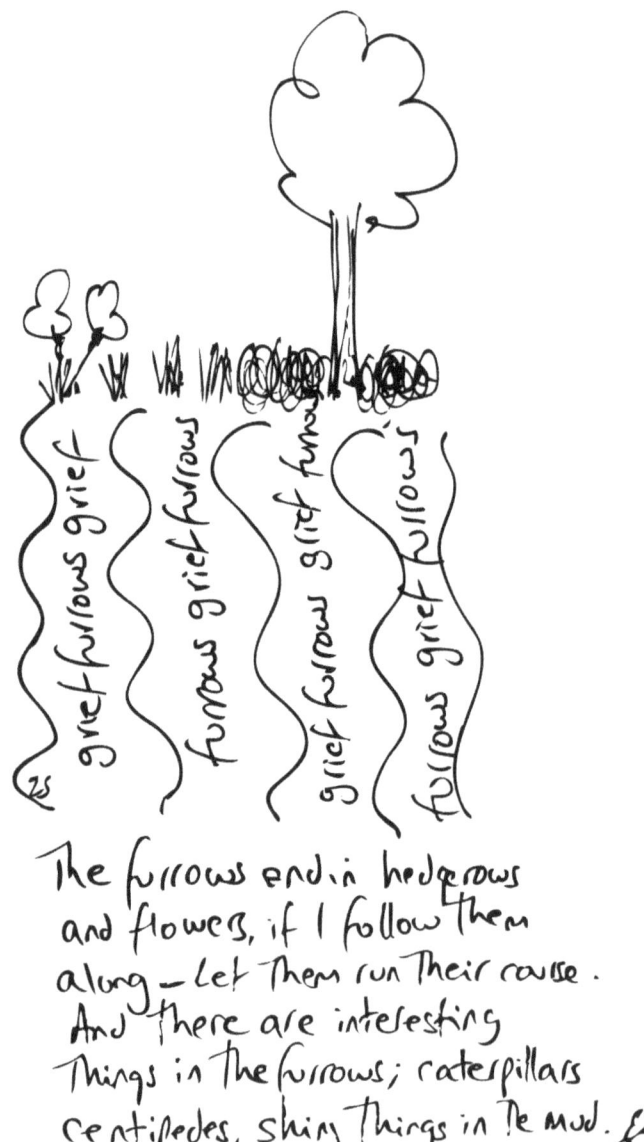

The furrows end in hedgerows
and flowers, if I follow them
along — let them run their course.
And there are interesting
things in the furrows; caterpillars
centipedes, shiny things in the mud.

Grief furrows

There have been several times when I've wondered, *Am I depressed?*

I think if I asked Grief, she would answer: "It's not depression dear, it's grief, dear."

I learned not to be afraid. The mud is soft and cool. It's quiet in there. A retreat from the fizz of external life and the exhausting heat of positivity. A place where seeds lie dormant in their blankety beds. There is much activity and life in those furrows—critters, caterpillars, snails, frogs. It's busy! Shiny treasure is waiting to be found.

I follow a furrow, let it run its course. It ends in hedgerows, trees, wildflowers, birds' nests. Renewal.

Black dog

brain fog

chest tightening

feels frightening.

But it's OKAY.

With one hand on my heart,

to anchor self-love,

partnering this feeling like a soothing glove,

the other on my belly

for comfort and ease

And "It's okay, I'm here for you …"

and with this, I breathe.

I remind myself

in this moment

this too shall pass

these difficult feelings don't usually last.

And soon enough,

there it is,

the positive chord from minor to major

a grounding rhythm heralded by nature,

the arc of the rainbow

a soft pink dawn

a beginning to the end

of the dark and the storm.

Where are you?

A midwife popped round today and recommended a little book, *The Light Between Us,* by Laura Lynne Jackson. I'm deeply immersed in its pages. From childhood, she realised she was a psychic medium. Her book shares, with such normalcy, her communion with the transitioned and the continuation of consciousness. She helped me better understand what I also felt … right there, right then. I shared this with Dad.

God bless midwives; they are witnesses to the sacred arrival and departure of souls. How did she know it was just what I needed right then?

little things that lift
like daffodils

Little things that lift

On a difficult day, a friend gave me daffodils.

Such an unexpected lift. Lasted all day.

Happy flowers, happy yellow.

We got married in a sea of daffodils. You were in my tummy.

I listen to Grief when she asks, "What do you need today, dear?"

Do more little things that lift

yoga

tai chi

Do more little things that lift

At yoga, gentle exercise helps me get out of my head and into my body. Connecting with my breath in steady standing poses, I do my level best to focus attention and embrace fluidity and acceptance. A grief warrior.

At tai chi, I sway

and rock

move my arms around ...

move chi

like an air bender

like an avatar.

Or I bash the bejeesuz out of the bongos ... and change up the vibration.

I kept my classes going. Oases of normalcy in the otherwise abnormal. A pocket of *right now, right here, I'm in my body and I'm okay.*

Stages of grief

Much has been written on the different stages of grief.

I deliberately avoided reading about them, opting for my own authentic experiences. But if I was asked to share, my list would include the following:

Coping

Opening

Learning

Growing

Finding Meaning

Divinity

Sometimes, like the weather, these all occur in one day, and possibly, divinity starting and finishing the list.

Faith

Faith alternates with doubt.

Doubt, with an open spirit, strengthens faith.

When we experience things for ourselves, we work things out, and faith becomes knowing.

For now, I hang on to faith ... that we will be okay ... so long as we stay in the love lane.

> *Doubt everything – find your own light.*
> —Buddha.

BRACE BRACE

birthdays, mothers day, fathers day, christmas day, anniversaries, so how many children do you have?

Brace brace

"So, what are you doing for Christmas?

How many children do you have?"

Birthdays, anniversaries, special days.

The first time you go to write a greeting card ... Love from ... it hurts so much to not write their name.

I read that it helps to rehearse some answers to tender questions. So, I did. Words that rolled off my tongue when caught off guard. Replies that didn't invite comment, because it varies so much on any given day whether you can cope with another person's sometimes unpredictable response. And are they ready for my full-frontal reply? Do I want to go there now? Can they hold the space for me, anyway?

Such innocuous day-to-day questions that send your mind into chaos.

TIPS:

For those who are not sure what to say to a person in early grief, whether you are meeting them for the first time, the second, or for the 100th time—because I know it's not easy.

"I'm sorry for your loss." You might feel this little phrase is overused, but it acknowledges your pain. Hearing this means a lot. More than you think.

"How are you, today?" Adding *today,* changes the feel of this simple question. Because, "How are you?" I mean where do you begin? And if we *are* feeling lighter, there's something about saying, "I'm okay, *today,* thanks," that acknowledges the fact that you are still grieving hard, and this might not have been so yesterday, might not be so tomorrow, and might not be in ten minutes.

Sound complicated? It is!

Quicksand

There are merciful pockets of ease,

And then …

Little things can set you right back. A song in the supermarket, a throwaway comment, a memory, the melancholy of the rain. A blue light, a passing ambulance, hauntingly silent.

The quicksand is uninvited and unexpected, though it's becoming less sticky as time goes on.

Making tea

A cup of tea is my 'go to', when it all gets too much. Comfort cupped in my hands, the warm steam on my face, and I almost fall in.

Tea slows me down. It's kind, dependable, and familiar. I don't have to do anything ... except have tea.

When the going gets tough, I go inside, close the door, and make tea.

> *Drink your tea slowly and reverently, as if it is the axis on which the earth revolves – slowly, evenly, without rushing toward the future.*
>
> —Thich Nhat Hanh.

Treading on eggshells

As a family, we made a pact that anyone could talk about anything at any time. To a large extent, we still do. But as time goes on, it does get tricky ... you don't want to upset anyone on a day that is going well for them.

How do you open a conversation if something is on your mind? When do you launch in? When is the right time? As time moves on, it can sometimes feel like you are treading on eggshells.

Oct 2018

The stars are comforting
sparkling in their trillions,
tiny pinpricks in the cosmos
where the love drips through.

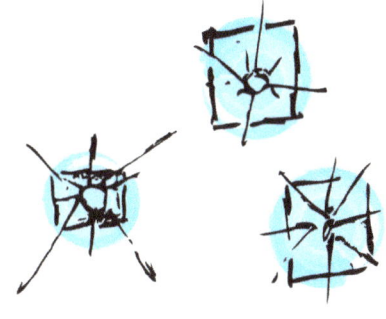

Fix your gaze and you lose them,
softening, they reappear,
blinking kindly in the infinite black.
They bring peace, a sense of hominess,
holiness.
And my soul feels safe resting in their yin.

star gazing

Okay

I get it

I've learned what I need

that'll do

Please come back now

I'll do anything you ask God,

if I can just see him again.

Even for one day a year.

Joy envy

Christmas build up ... I have joy envy.

I wish I didn't feel so sad. I just miss you.

A tidal wave comes over—a swoon of grief, like my legs want to give way; a pounding in my head; a knot in my throat. If I just hold my breath, I'll be able to hold back the tsunami. I jiggle my leg, tap my fingers, go to the loo ... again!

I feel socially numb, inept, uninteresting and uninterested—even among people who care deeply for me.

People notice ... edgy eyes ... they try to make polite conversation. Please, nobody ask if I'm okay. Don't touch me. Don't hug me. Let me be present, but let me be invisible.

P.S. Reminder: Be kind to self. I'm in early grief.

Thanks to the special people in my life, and my family, who continue to show up and expect nothing.

Chit chat chit chat

spewing banalities, this and that

for how can I really say

the things on my mind

the state of play

the seething undertow of pain

now, tomorrow, every day.

Perhaps I'll take a vow of silence

it might be better that way.

I practice social quarantine, so I don't have to relate to others.

I'm fine in my own home zone.

suicide
#KillingThestigma

I'm ready for that comment
I wonder when it's coming
and then it does -
It's so selfish suicide isn't it?

Boxing gloves

Though I was ready, I felt enraged.

Right from the start, I have instinctively felt that suicide is not selfish. An act of self, by the self, for the self, but not selfish. Tragic, not selfish. Not in a good mindset, not selfish. Split from self? Not selfish. Suicide is a behaviour, acted out in emotional overwhelm, when other options are not seen.

I would have done every single possible thing in my power, for this not to have happened. But it did. And because I honour him with total unconditional love, I accept his choice totally free of judgement. Suicide is one part of an individuals' story—it does not define their life, their beliefs, their values, or their love.

Please educate people when they say suicide is selfish. And remind them to use the terminology—they 'died by suicide' not, 'committed suicide', because this hails from a time when suicide was considered a crime and a sin.

As a family, we align ourselves with charitable organisations and events that support mental health and provide education on suicide awareness and prevention.

#killingthestigma

#suicideawarenessprevention

Hollow

The hollowness is a melancholy ache.

Like Boo Radley, I bring offerings to my hollow. Trinkets of you: your little red glass Buddha, a coin, your pen, a green marble. Yoda's there, and a dinosaur. They sit on your table with a photo, slightly tucked behind a vase—because, right now, it's too hard to look full on.

Nature's offerings sit there too: feathers that find me, seed pods, stones, shells, crystals. I collect them like a bowerbird. Make offerings. Light a candle. They comfort.

We feel you in this, and your approval.

To be or not to be
That is the question.

I confess I have thought about it … joining you.

I looked it in the eye fleetingly. A dark but hallowed moment, because I understood right then how you felt. It was all about me, nothing to do with anyone else, no one's fault, no one to blame, it was just about me, the exit door from overwhelming pain, ajar. I get it.

When you are thinking about wanting to die, you are also questioning why you want to live. In my mind, I wrote two lists. A sobering no-brainer.

Always write two lists.

Plug into earthly life, earthly love—it matters, you matter.

Keep walking.

This too will pass.

It will pass.

Knowing your own darkness is the best method for dealing with the darknesses of other people. One does not become enlightened by imagining figures of light but by making the dark conscious.

—Carl Jung.

Dark nights of the soul are when I hone my night vision.

Night vision

There is much to be done during your dark night which is full of mysteries. Your job is to take care not to interfere with the work being done, by bringing your day time biases to it. Let night be night. It has proper spirits ... its tools, and its tough workers.

—Thomas Moore, *Dark Nights of the Soul.*

Hunter Moon
Up she rises
and as she does
my emotional chaos

benevolent or malevolent?
not sure …
but she pulls me into her beam
out 'there'
where the eagles are
into the slip stream
… and the gate is open.

Though mind over moon,
I choose instead
to stay in bed and write.
The eagles cry,
the tree frogs call,
the bush turkeys warble,
rippling the stillness,
and her white light
fills my mind
with peaceful nothing.

I beg for sleep,
She grants it
And dawn nudges her away
easing me into another day.

May, please stay

May 2019

I want it to be May forever. It's like I'm free falling to 23 June. It's your first anniversary, Elliot. I could unravel … nauseous and anxious again … re-reading texts. What did I miss? I want to forget. I want to remember.

Shall I organise a get together? What to do? What's appropriate? What do others want? Do they want to come? How can we possibly celebrate the day of your passing? But we can't just have dinner, watch telly, and go to bed. It feels like I'm leaving you behind. I feel such pressure to be 'normal', as time goes on.

Time heals. How I hate that expression!

And the gate was open. I drove past and had to return. To stand on the spot where I last held you—your physical life newly dissolved in my arms; the sense of you so strong. You were not there … but you so were. And as I thought this, I felt the brush of your face in the breeze,

I kissed my hand and touched the ground.

You came to me,

whispered some suggestions into my dreaming …

I went home to share

and it all worked out perfectly.

Thanks, darling.

May 2023

Five years on

Your body doesn't lie. It's interesting how your body seems to remember that a sorrowful anniversary is coming up.

Emotions more wobbly, tears spring randomly. Maybe like birds just 'know' when to migrate, or fly home to the exact same spot to nest, or whales start their journey to the north.

A body clock, a feeling that builds. I honour the grief that I, and we all carry, and I remind myself to stay in the love lane.

Alice: How long is forever?

White Rabbit: Sometimes just one second.

—Lewis Carroll, *Alice's Adventures in Wonderland.*

On longing

Intellectually and somewhere on the outer edges of my soul

I can accept death

that death is a part of life

that in befriending death, we grow in life …

that life involves suffering

that growth involves suffering

that all things must pass

that endings are beginnings.

I respect that we all have a choice

and I will accept that choice

but despite all this

sometimes the longing feels like forever

and forever feels like a long time.

> *And I saw the river over which every soul must pass to reach the Kingdom of Heaven, and the name of that river was suffering. And I saw a boat which carries souls across the river, and the name of that boat was love.*
>
> —St John of the Cross.

Beautiful, beautiful bird,

you sit so serenely on your watch tower

watching me, watching you.

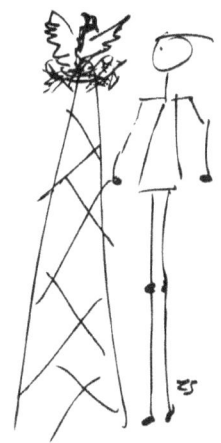

Beautiful, beautiful boy,

penny for 'em

as you sit atop your twiggy throne,

what secrets do you keep?

Loving me loving you?

Dear Eagle,

I am soothed and mesmerised by your circling,

and as your wings catch the updraft,

so do I.

I listen to the whisperings of my soul,

soaring up high

where eagles dare,

if you're brave enough to listen,

I'm brave enough to share.

Your anniversary

June 23 2019

Darling Elliot, on the night of your blessing gathering, we felt suspended in a state of grace and ease. We drifted through an evening that you would have loved, and we felt you there. We trusted we would find the right way to remember you, and we did. A strawberry sunset on a tropical beach with your friends, a fire pit, rousing singing and simultaneous silence. We cried a lot; we laughed a lot. Dad made gallons of home brew.

A huge moon ballooned up from the ocean into a heavenly sky, and at the pub we were randomly given table number 23—of course!

You were created by love, you were born in love, you lived in love, you left us in love, you left us with love, you are love, together we are bound in love, for always.

The actual day of his first anniversary was sweeter than the build-up. Others report the same. If we can move through grief with love, everything is possible. An awakening to an intense love of a spiritual kind is the kind of love that helps us trust ourselves.

On talking to eagles

It's been fourteen months and I still feel like I'm in a relationship with him. A close one. A real one. We talk daily. I chat out loud in the park. I am relieved to know this is normal and healthy.

Eagle is his spirit animal. There is an eyrie close to home, close to the place of his passing. An eagle appeared very soon after his transition. They revisit the nest every year. Eagles continue to appear for all of us that are close to him. They show up at special times. Times when we've felt like we just can't go on, times of doubt, of celebration, unusual places. Once, right in the middle of the road on a really hard day.

Eagles bring comfort and connection. I have read that the spirit world finds it easier to connect with human spiritual beginners through animals.

And sometimes

despite the love and the light

the sunshine and the flowers

the knowing and the growing

it all feels like

this.

Secret world

Grief is like having a secret world. Like living Karma in real time. A parallel universe. It's like your other life. An air of normalcy as you go about your day, but there's a whole lot else going on alongside, "Yes, I'm doing fine, thanks. How are you?"

A world where I play my singing bowl, or I lie down and imagine a portal opening up above me where I join him. The real world and the secret world meeting over an expresso martini.

A world where my mind is constantly with him—both in memories and in the life, I imagine for him now.

A secret world where I curl up in his clothes, breath him in, immerse myself in hours of photos, write to him, revisit texts … how can it be that I think about him even more now?

I learn to walk in two worlds. And I wonder, *How many others are doing the same … in their parallel universes?*

Sometimes, I wonder which one is more real.

So I stand up

step into the dreaming

into the liminal space

hold my arms in a loving circle

and he steps into my hug.

Medicinal marijuana

lifts my right brain out of my left brain …

relaxation response

a pleasant filminess

deep belly laughs.

My body remembering laughing,

letting go into laughter,

which goes where it goes.

I haven't laughed like this for 17 months.

Shared giggling at nothing, at everything,

satisfyingly exhausting

a lightness of spirit,

body - light

deep rest.

#griefhurts

But when the grief-fog clears, after a year, or two, or three,

the clarity is sharp and pointy.

It's hard, day-by-day, to stay seeing with the heart.

#havingabadday

padded quilt skies
fill my mind with you
fairweather thoughts
a soul kiss
spiritual connection
pockets of bliss

You know, a good friend of mine said you are married to sorrow and I looked to him and I said, I'm not married to sorrow, I just choose not to look away. And I think there is a deep beauty in not diverting our gaze. No matter how heartbreaking it can be, I think it's about presence, bearing witness. I used to think that bearing witness was a passive act. I don't believe that anymore. I think that when we are present, when we bear witness and we are present, when we do not divert our gaze, something is revealed. The very marrow of life. We change. A transformation occurs. A consciousness shift.

—Terry Tempest Williams, *Finding Beauty in a Broken World.*

Coroner's letters ... I wish they could all be hand-delivered by angels.

Coroner's letter

Eighteen months

At first, you can't cry … too much pain for tears. Then it builds. A bit like not wanting to vomit, but you can't hold it back … it's coming, and then it does.

Deep, guttural cries I hardly recognise.

My face contorts into *'The Scream'*.

The waves come, like birth cries, each wave stronger,

more and more intense,

reaching a peak; I thought I would burst and not come back.

I let go, fell into it, almost relishing it,

nothing can feel worse now.

Then slowly coming down

like a wave,

storm subsiding,

… my breath—so slow, so shallow. Am I still breathing?

My muscles ache,

I could sleep forever.

I melt in the aftermath,

It's good to cry.

Blessed release.

After a rest, I felt better. Carried on with some gentle chores and did some vacuuming. I was even hungry. My husband and I enjoyed an evening walk together with our dog, bought a newspaper from our happy village grocery store, bought a 'scratchie' and won $3!

I wondered how many other people received their coroner's letters today. It seems so cruel you never know when it's coming. Right out of the blue and up to eighteen months after. I guess they are busy.

I wish they could be hand-delivered by angels.

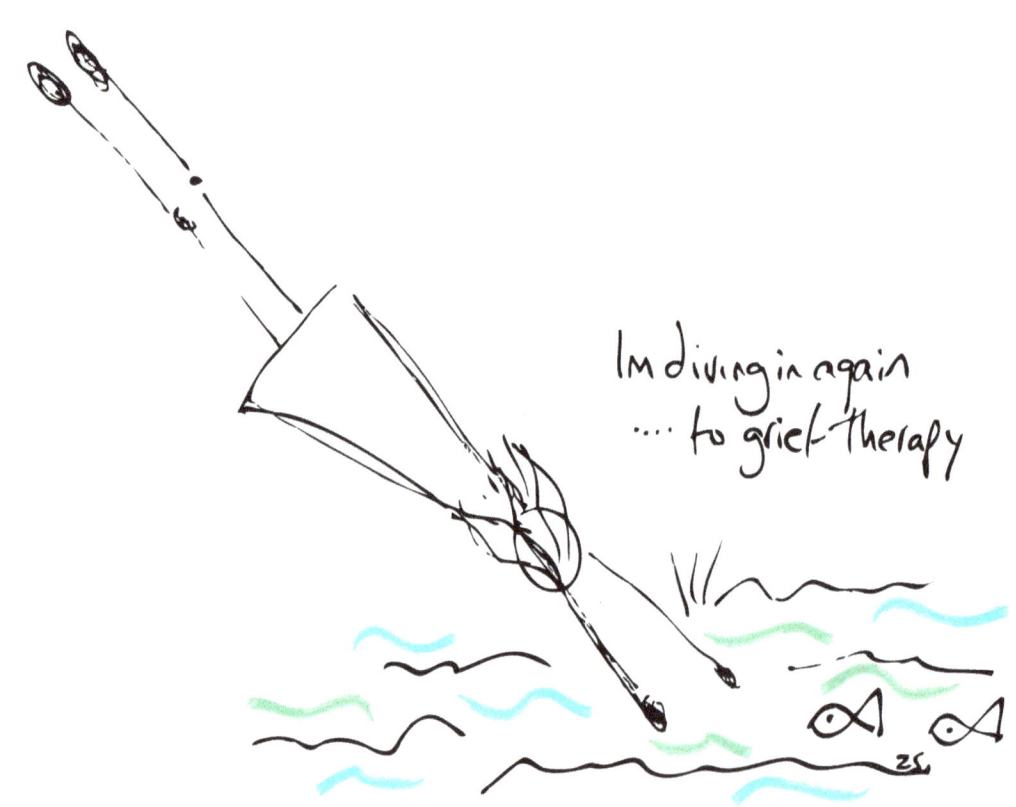

Diving back into therapy

Someone asked me what makes a great therapist, and I'm not exactly sure. It's a kind of soul-to-soul conversation. A suggestion of what the heart might need. A reminder to notice what helps and what doesn't. A reminder to ask Grief what she needs today.

I suspect that the magic that happens in therapy goes beyond clinical practice. Perhaps it's a meeting at the crossroads of psychology and spirituality. It's about connection, finding the right fit. Healing is definitely a two-way process.

There is a fogginess in early grief that buffers the detail. After about eighteen months, it wears off, and the clarity comes back painfully sharp and pointy. I resumed psychotherapy sessions with my therapist. EMDR, in particular, helped soften the edges.

I dive back in, so I can safely let it out, making space for the letting in, as she looks at me with kind eyes. "Yes, yes," and with deep listening nods, "good work."

unhelpful ☹	helpful ☺
Move on ✗	Move along ✓
let go ✗	let in ✓
be brave ✗	be real ✓

I don't want to move on, let go, or be brave.

Moving along, letting in, being real, feels better.

what makes it better?
connecting with nature

On nature

Grief doesn't like to be cornered.

Being out in nature gives her space to breathe, a feeling of expansiveness. We are organic beings. We feel better in nature. Our spirit rests easier here. Natural Law contains it all; harshness, changeability, and chaos. There is also comfort and predictability, found in repetitive pattern forms and golden ratios. There is death, there is sleeping, there is rebirth. The natural world has a pulse … an awesomeness … that's bigger than ourselves.

I feel the steady wisdom of a tree at my back,

and the groundedness of the earth under my feet.

I allow in the cheerfulness of birdsong,

and a cool wind to refresh my energy.

The fluid element of water carries my stream of consciousness,

the swash and the backwash of the ocean keep it all moving,

there is a goodness to Mother Nature … I find solace here.

> *Keep a green bough in your heart and the singing bird will come.*
> —Chinese proverb.

Lightness of being

Yes, even in amongst it all, you can feel like this.

A heady sense of lightness.

It happens.

I sincerely wish everyone, a lightness of being.

If you keep doing the same,

you get the same.

Change is okay when you are ready.

I open my arms to the
stars and feel my
imaginary wings unfold

And as I do ... I feel myself as a bird

Light like feathers

And we fly together.

It feels good

To fly as fast as thought, to anywhere that is,
you must begin by knowing that you have already arrived.
—Richard Bach, *Jonathan Livingston Seagull.*

Magic happens

Sometime in the first year of grief and loss, and I'm not sure why, I started to make crystal wands. Also, little people, wood spirits, twig angels, dryads, and sky dancers. I foraged for materials, collecting feathers, timber, and local flora to dry and bind. I made smudge bundles for ritual burnings. At about the same time, I was introduced to Druid philosophy. I found much that made sense in this nature- based spirituality.

Perhaps it was about making connections with the unseen but felt energies in nature, and in doing so, bringing about change within myself. Perhaps it was an instinctive turning to the healing vibrations of nature. Perhaps it was because I just needed to believe in magic. But the wands … they seemed to start making themselves. The stick found me, a crystal chose the stick. I pared it, sanded it, branded it with a fire tool, and bound feathers and charms to the shaft. I adorned it with silver or copper, hemp, and leather. Each wand seemed to come together as a story, gained momentum, and became greater than the sum of its parts. And I found organisation in what appeared to be random.

It became an obsession. For hours and days, I lost myself (or maybe found myself) and it felt good. I invited Elliot's friends to make a healing wand with me, and special moments were shared around the kitchen table. I made them as gifts for friends and family, and then one day, I received an order! What had been self-enforced seclusion in a hobby turned into much more.

Wisdom Wands was born. And I started to run wand-making grief workshops. Magic happened. Magic is happening.

> *And above all, watch with glittering eyes the whole world around you, because the greatest secrets are always hidden in the most unlikely places. Those who don't believe in magic will never find it.*
>
> —Roald Dahl, *The Minpins.*

When the skin has been ripped off your bones,

and you have shed your skin,

it can leave you raw and exposed.

Your underbelly is soft and tender and needs to undergo repair.

Keep your heart open—but take care who you let in.

I acknowledge the suffering
that others are surely feeling
grateful for the good feelings I
never thought possible
and the transience of all things.
zs

Grief … it's not just a spiritual trip, you have to do the work, work, work.

Despite all the support, of which there is plenty, there are no shortcuts. A lot of our work is an inside job. It's often lonely and exhausting in the undertow, but we have to do it.

Dear Self,

today I affirm,

I won't fall apart.

My husband loves and needs me.

My boys love and need me.

Chubbs, our dog, loves and needs me.

My family loves me, and I love them.

I have good friends.

I can contribute to my family's healing.

I am learning ways to move through my own trauma.

I share my thoughts and feelings, and this might help others walking in my shoes.

I do meaningful work and can do things that make a difference.

I deserve a rich and meaningful life; he would want THIS for me.

I want this for me.

People say I'm brave.

I don't feel brave,

I'm just doing life as best I can each day.

I strive to find happiness and contentment

where I am.

A terrible thing has happened

but I try not to let this cloud who I am at my core.

And what if …

right at our core,

where the steady earth

meets the spaciousness of the sky,

everything is well,

everything is whole,

whole and unbroken.

A touch stone,

a place where we can go

in our needing.

Kintsugi

Elliot, we have a plant pot of yours; it broke, and I was upset.

A friend of yours told me today about Kintsugi. I hadn't heard of it before so, I googled …

"The unique, and centuries-old Japanese art of repairing broken pottery with lacquer dusted with gold. An enchanting art that highlights the fractures and breaks in its life, instead of hiding or disguising them. The repaired piece is even more beautiful than the original."

Dad and I took our time and carefully mended your pot with glue and gold dust. We planted it with red geraniums. It looks lovely.

I embrace Kintsugi and repair my own broken pieces with gold.

Here comes the moon, the moon, the moon, the moon, the moon.

A flower moon in May

she wraps me in a silver hug

and whissssssspers,

"Stay with me tonight,

I'll see the sun walks you home when it's light."

Making friends with the moon

I thought I'd share a bit more about this diary entry.

It took me a long time to make friends with the moon, to feel safe in the dark, in the presence of her tug. For the first time in a long while, I felt bathed in a more benevolent moonlight. I felt less hollow in the still of the dark.

It was a full-moon night. My husband was playing George Harrison's sweet song, *Here Comes the Moon* (the moon, the moon, the moon, the moon), in the background. We named Elliot after the little boy in the film, *E.T. the Extra-Terrestrial*, which has always been a favourite of ours.

I was moved to write, and my pen started to doodle.

Doodle Lady's entry was an invitation to myself, as well as to others, to stay safe in the night and feel more peace. A time when we can often feel the most despair. It is an unconscious and plaintive wishing that Elliot had stayed with the moon that night, till she walked him home in the morn.

Such is the catharsis that happens through journaling. Such an unpeeling of layers. Such revelation. I wholeheartedly recommend it.

Let your heart, your grief, your psyche pick up a pen. Write to your former self, your now self, your future self. Write to them, write poems, fill a page with expletives. My nana always said, "Better out than in, dear."

I really recommend journaling as self-directed therapy to help shape and assimilate the pain of grief.

New Year, January 1st 2022

I've never been a big fan of Happy New Year hype. And now, each turning of the wheel puts more distance between our last hug. I prefer, "Start Where You Are." You can do that on any day of the year. Wherever you are, you can always start ... just where you are.

A letter to suffering

Dear Suffering,

I wish you honey balm for your cuts,

an immediate loosening of the noose that holds you,

the softest of landings for your fall.

I wish you sweet medicine for your dis-ease

humming bird nectar for your poison

and a laying down of all weapons.

I wish you water wings for your drowning,

a reunion with the highest intention of your soul

I wish you deep rest in your angst.

I wish you the light of the Holy Spirit

to see universal wisdoms in your confusion

A lavender eye mask for sights rather not seen,

fleece earmuffs to pad the sounds of your crying.

I summon a warm zephyr,

to greet your heart and to waft your inner pilot light,

and the wind elves to carry your song into the ethers

and magically receive their messages.

Dear Suffering, I wish you peace in your dreaming,

may you offer and receive unconditional love,

may you live in love,

may your dying be in love.

Laundry

And so, where am I now?

It's less complicated … I just miss him.

I bring this work to a close, and though it's never finished, equally there's a point when I know where to stop.

Looking back through my diaries, I feel like I've travelled far. Grief is often present in my head, and resident in my heart, but it no longer sinks me.

It's like the laundry. I do it most days … some days a light load, others a heavier wash. But I can hang her out to air, let her waft gently in the breeze, gather her in, fold her up and carry her.

I gave my grief to Doodle Lady to share, so it didn't own me. Perhaps in sharing my diaries, we are ready to become one now. And perhaps that's where new learning begins.

Postlude

For dear Grief,

it's not time that heals, is it?

It's honesty,

it's a relationship,

a transitional place where we get to know each other

intimately.

There is no finale,

more cadences

endings suggesting beginnings,

where I care for your needs

and tend to my human heart whilst it adjusts to your physical loss

and moves me to the felt experience of you

where you become alive to me in so many other ways.

Resources

From my Reading List

It's OK That You're Not OK – Megan Devine

The Light Between Us – Laura Lynne Jackson

Dark Night of The Soul – Thomas Moore

Many Lives Many Masters – Brian Weiss

There Are No Goodbyes – Elizabeth Robinson

The Five Invitations. Discovering What Death Can Teach Us About Living Fully – Frank Otaseski

The Deep Heart Our Portal to Presence – John Prendergast

Phosphoresence: On Awe, Wonder and Things That Sustain You When The World Goes Dark – Julia Baird

Intimate Conversations With The Divine Prayer Guidance And Grace – Caroline Myss

Anam Cara A Book of Spiritual Celtic Wisdom – John O'Donohue

Meditations, mindfulness, and spiritual teachers

Jack Kornfield – assorted texts, posts, and heart- based mindfulness courses.

Tich Nhat Hanh. Vietnamese monk, peace activist, teacher of active Buddhism, assorted works and *The Great Bell Chant*.

Sadhguru – Indian yoga guru and spiritual teacher.

Moola Mantra Incantation – A powerful mantra and lullaby for the soul, transporting one's mind to a state of calm and boundless love. An invocation of the living presence of God, asking for protection and freedom from sorrow and suffering.

Mooji – Jamaican spiritual teacher, poet, writer, and meditation teacher.

Philip Carr- Gomm – author, psychologist, spiritual leader, poet, meditation teacher, sophrologist, founder of the order of Bards, Ovates and Druids. *Tea with a druid* podcasts.

Other learnings

Talk Safe, Plan Safe, suicide awareness prevention training – The OLLIE Foundation, Hertfordshire, UK.

The Elliot Strickland Lecture for goal setting for mental health and suicide ideation – www.theolliefoundation.org.

Mental Health First Aid Australia – mhfa.com.au.

Acknowledgements

It takes a village to support a person and their family through loss. I would like to acknowledge the following people, and all their kindnesses, who have been so instrumental in helping us on the road to recovery. In no particular hierarchical order, THANK YOU:

Jo, my psychotherapist, our funeral celebrant and now dear friend.

Our special Debbie in Atherton.

Our special Debi in Hertfordshire, long-time friend and CEO at The Ollie Foundation.org

Dagmar, my yoga teacher—for her gentle wisdoms and sharing the Moola Mantra Invocation.

Our friends in the Cairns community; you are too numerous to mention, but you know who you are. For checking in with us, bringing us food, flowers, partnering us in our new normal. We really felt held by our workmates, neighbours, football parents, camping buddies, school parents, musos, scrabble partners!

Amanda and John, our local GPs; you were right there from day one.

Elliot's friends. Thank you for staying close to us, sharing stories, making the most beautiful remembrance video and your continued connection with our family.

Tama and associates for receiving Elliot and sending him on his way to heaven. We couldn't have imagined a more beautiful soul to do this.

Nick, my husband's long time school friend, for your extraordinary gift of love, and time; for getting on a plane from the UK on day three, and visiting us on the other side of the planet for two days. Such a profound comfort to David, and our family, in the trenches.

The Red Beret Hotel for hosting an uplifting and rousing wake for us all when we were too frazzled to even think about organising one.

My clients for continuing to book in and trust me with my pre-natal natural therapy services and meditation courses. For their sharing and book recommendations; one's clients so often become one's teachers.

Anne from Compassionate Friends, for your early support at all hours on Messenger and your own sharing.

Rob in Christchurch; a young man, suicide survivor and advocate for suicide awareness prevention, for inspiring us to host a Let's Chalk about Mental Health Australia annual event. You helped us to find meaning in the undertow. Thank you to the people who came and chalked and shared their stories on the path.

Sharnie from ABC, for making a powerfully tender video *about our Let's Chalk about Mental Health event*, that went viral, and sparked similar events around Australia and overseas.

Our dear long-time friends in the UK, and our special Barnet walk-to-school community. We don't see you much, but the connection and love between our families runs deep.

Sarah, for your exquisite portrait of Elliot; he literally breathes off the canvas.

My spiritual and professional teachers, both personal and online, for helping me look at things differently, and assimilate life learnings in a real way: Marilyn, for your magical reframes; Jack Kornfield, for your compassionate, heart-based mindfulness; and the Sounds True community of healers and writers.

My friends, for liking my Doodle Lady posts! For encouraging me to continue posting her musings, for reading and commenting on my manuscript, and nudging me to publish.

Melissa, for all your help with my graphics and getting the vectors ready, wave after wave.

Our new Sunshine Coast community, for supporting my grief workshops, wand-making and crafting circles.

My editor angel, Kym Fullerton. For pouring herself into every word, for our journeying together.

Mother Nature: for your trees and your steady wisdoms, for the uplift of your oceans and waves, for upside down skies and panoramic sands, for birds and your songs, for the warming sun, for life-giving waters, the gentle stars, the benevolent moon, and the cheerfulness of flowers.

Thank you to our family—ALL of you—brothers, sisters, partners, nieces, nephews. Thank you for leaning in, for your love, your visits to Australia, getting in our lane with us, your care, your bravery, your advocacy and fundraising, your tenderness and practical support. Thank you for choosing Elliot's name in the naming of your babies.

Mark – for helping us navigate those gut wrenching early practicalities, and our peaceful, stone Buddha. He sits reading under a tree and continues to calm our soul.

Mary Poppins—both real and fictional.

Mum and Dad for your unconditional love. Mum, though it was all too hard to talk about, I treasure your embroidered tear catchers and to Dad for reading my manuscript and saying it was good!

Elliot, for your love, your special gifts, for being you and being in our midst, always.

Angels and heavenly hosts, that we are blessed to feel around us, and the Great Spirit which so often has our back.

Chubbs for your unconditional love, and wagging tail; it is a windmill of joy.

Thank you David, Jacob, and Freddy. I can't quite articulate the continued deep love, trust, and support I feel from you now, and every single day, so I'll blow you a kiss instead x

And thank you to YOU for buying this book. It means a lot.

Zoe Strickland grew up in East Yorkshire, lived her adult life in North London, and immigrated with her husband and three boys to Australia in 2007. She became a natural therapies practitioner, living and working in the tropical Cairns community, teaching hypno-birthing and mindfulness meditation. After her loss, Zoe found solace in living life in the slow lane and followed creative and intuitive pursuits. She facilitates grief workshops and a shared love of wand making. In 2023, she became a qualified florist, finding joy in flowering beginnings, endings and everything in between.

Zoe is now a proud grandma, and lives with her husband, and dog Chubbs, on the beautiful Sunshine Coast in Queensland, near to her children.

www.ingramcontent.com/pod-product-compliance
Lightning Source LLC
Chambersburg PA
CBHW042358070526
44585CB00029B/2980